51 things to make with
Cardboard Boxes

Fiona Hayes

Contents

Basic Equipment

Most of these projects use some or all of the following equipment, so keep these handy:

- **White glue**
- **Scissors**
- **Pencils**
- **Ruler**
- **Felt-tip pens**
- **Paintbrushes**

Giraffe

This gorgeous giraffe will look great in your bedroom. Why not make two and use them as bookends?

You will need

Two cereal boxes

Three long boxes

Brown, yellow, pink, and green paint

Brown cardboard

Thin cardstock

Two googly eyes

One yellow straw

1

Cut the end off a cereal box to make the body. Glue two long boxes inside the body box to make legs.

2

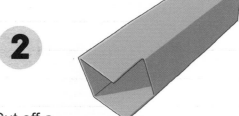

Cut off a section from one end of another long box to make the neck.

3

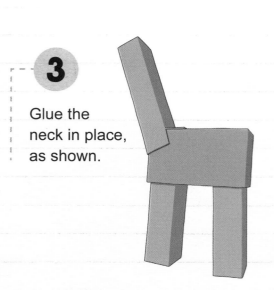

Glue the neck in place, as shown.

4

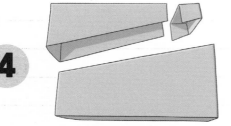

Cut a wedge from another cereal box, as shown. This top part will be the head. Recycle the rest of the box.

5

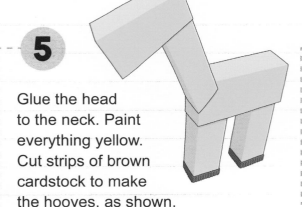

Glue the head to the neck. Paint everything yellow. Cut strips of brown cardstock to make the hooves, as shown.

6

Cut out a pair of ears from cardstock, paint them yellow, and glue them in place. Paint on lots of brown spots.

7

Cut a rectangle of brown cardboard to cover the snout. Then cut a strip to make the mane and some for the tail. Cut circles of thin cardstock and paint green. Glue the eyes to the green circles and fix to the head. Cut two short pieces of straw for horns. Paint details such as a smile. Add pink to the ears to finish your giraffe.

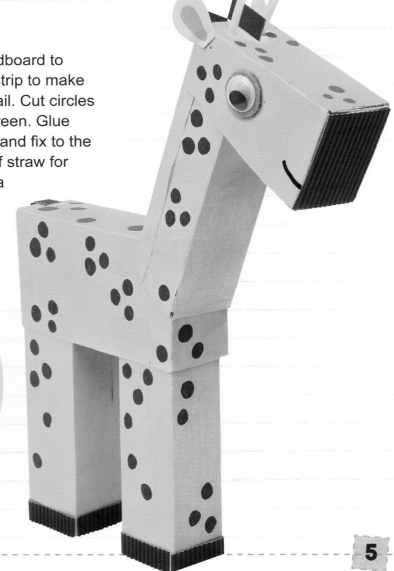

Handy Hint
For stand-out eyes, cut circles slightly bigger than the googly eyes. Paint them a bright color and glue the eyes to the circles.

Crocodile

Never smile at a crocodile—
unless it is as cute as this
spotted croc!

1

Cut the corner
off a box.

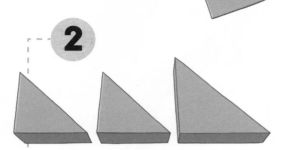

2

Cut off another two small corners
so that you have three triangles.

3

Cut the sides off another
box, as shown.

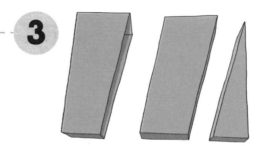

4

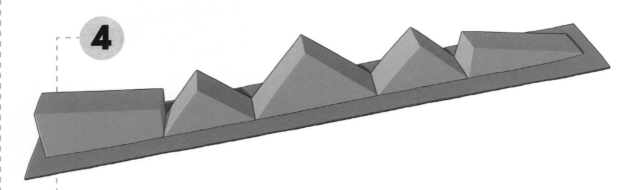

Paint all the pieces green. Cut a piece of cardboard
long enough to fit the crocodile body parts and
paint it. Glue the pieces to the cardboard.

5

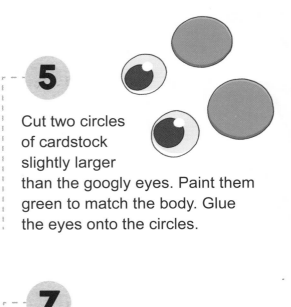

Cut two circles of cardstock slightly larger than the googly eyes. Paint them green to match the body. Glue the eyes onto the circles.

6

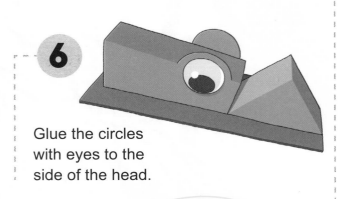

Glue the circles with eyes to the side of the head.

7

Paint on some spots and nostrils. Snap...snap… your amazing croc is ready!

Handy Hint
Make sure the paint is completely dry before painting on the details.

SNAP

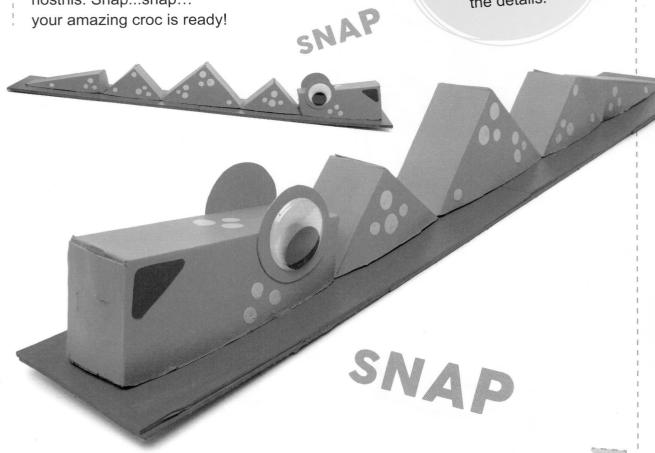

SNAP

Beetle Cars

Beep! Beep! It's time to take these beetle cars for a drive.

You will need

One round box
Paint, including black, blue, and white
Cardboard

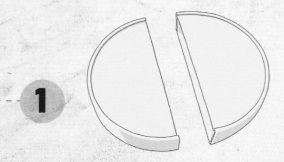

1 Glue the lid of the round box to the box base. Cut the box in half to make two car bodies.

2 Cut out four circles from cardboard. Paint them to look like wheels.

3 Paint the body of each car. When dry, paint two windows on either side.

4 Glue the wheels in place. Vroom, vroom! These little cars make great toys for rainy days!

8

Pirate Hat

Arrggh...me hearties! Impress all your friends with your pirate hat!

You will need

Large cereal box
Black paint
White cardstock

1

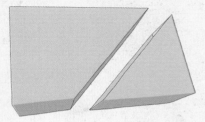

Cut the corner off a large cereal box.

2

Paint the corner black and recycle the rest.

3

Cut out a circle and a pair of bones from white cardstock to make a skull and crossbones.

4

Draw a face on the skull. Stick the skull and bones to the front of the hat, as shown. Why not make an eye patch to complete your pirate look?

Train

Choo, choo! All aboard! This colorful train will look great on your bedroom windowsill.

1

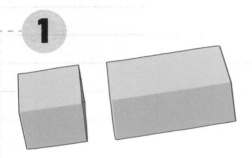

Cut a long box in two, as shown.

2

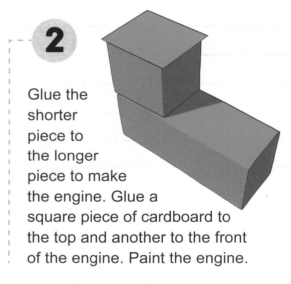

Glue the shorter piece to the longer piece to make the engine. Glue a square piece of cardboard to the top and another to the front of the engine. Paint the engine.

3

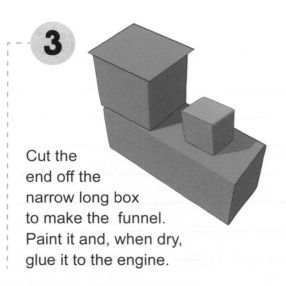

Cut the end off the narrow long box to make the funnel. Paint it and, when dry, glue it to the engine.

4

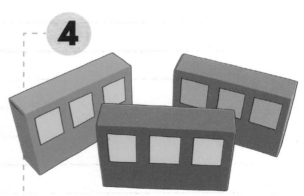

Paint some mini cereal boxes for the carriages. Paint on some windows.

5

Glue on some bottle tops
for the wheels. If you do not
have bottle tops, cut out
circles of cardstock instead.

6

Glue lengths of ribbon
to the base of the carriages
and engine to join them.

7

Choo, choo! Your train is
ready to leave the station!

CHOO CHOO

Flamingo

What's bright pink, feathery, and lives in Africa? A flamingo!

You will need

One cereal box
Two long boxes
One small box
Cardstock

Pink, white, black, and yellow paint
Two googly eyes

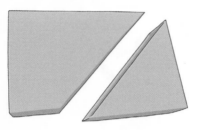

Cut the corner off a large cereal box.

Cut another triangular section from the rest of the box. Use the corner you cut in step 1 as a template.

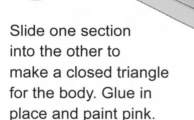

Slide one section into the other to make a closed triangle for the body. Glue in place and paint pink.

Cut out a triangular section from the end of each long box. These will be the neck and legs.

Cut the end off a smaller box to make a head. Glue the neck box in place. Paint the neck and part of the head pink. Give the flamingo a white and black beak.

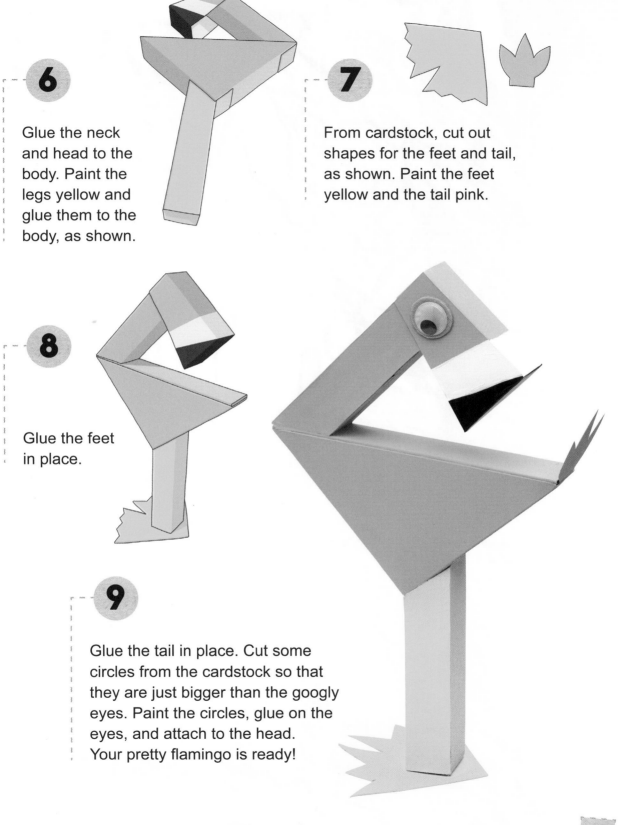

6

Glue the neck and head to the body. Paint the legs yellow and glue them to the body, as shown.

7

From cardstock, cut out shapes for the feet and tail, as shown. Paint the feet yellow and the tail pink.

8

Glue the feet in place.

9

Glue the tail in place. Cut some circles from the cardstock so that they are just bigger than the googly eyes. Paint the circles, glue on the eyes, and attach to the head. Your pretty flamingo is ready!

Hippo

Hippos love to wade in water—
except for this one!

You will need

Two small boxes

Six matchboxes

Paper clips

**Dark pink, light pink,
green, and white paint**

White cardstock

Googly eyes

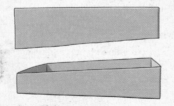

1

Cut a small box in half, as
shown. This will be the head.

2

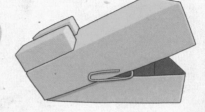

Glue two
matchboxes for
eyes to the top of
one of the pieces.
Paint both parts
of the head light
pink on the outside
and dark pink on the inside.

3

Glue the backs of the boxes
together, making sure you have
the mouth open. Use some
paper clips to hold the pieces
in place until they are dry.

4

Paint another box light pink.
Glue this to the back of the head.

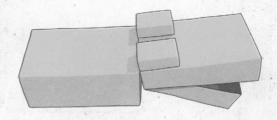

5

Paint four matchboxes light pink and
glue them to the bottom for feet.

6

Cut out a pair of ears from cardstock and paint light pink, with dark pink in the inside.

Handy Hint

If you do not have pink paint, you could mix red and white to get the right shade.

7

Cut some circles from the cardstock so that they are just bigger than the googly eyes. Paint the circles green, glue on the eyes, and attach to the head. Glue on the ears. Cut out some teeth from the white cardstock and glue them inside the mouth.

8

Paint on some spots, nostrils, and toenails. Say hello to your grinning hippo!

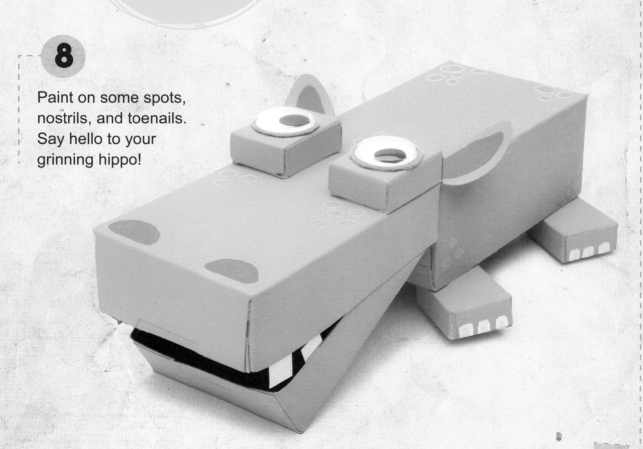

15

Truck

vrooom...Beep, beep! Watch out. This huge truck is carrying a heavy load!

1

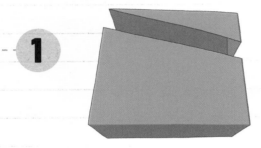

Cut the top off a box at an angle, as shown. The large piece will be the trailer of your truck.

2

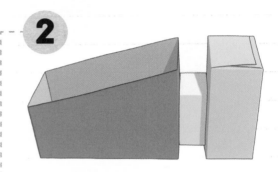

Find a box the same height as your trailer for the driver's cab. Glue a small box between the cab and trailer, as shown. Paint all pieces.

3

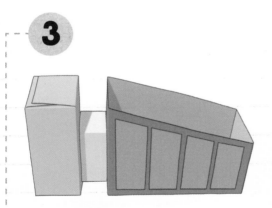

Cut some panels from the corrugated cardstock. Paint them and glue them to the trailer.

4

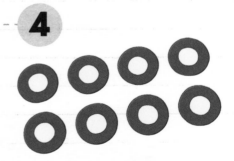

Cut out eight circles from cardboard and paint them black. Glue some smaller circles of shiny cardstock to the centers.

5

Glue the wheels in place. Cut out some windows from cardstock and glue to the cab.

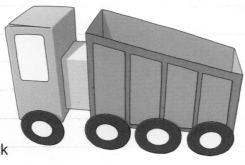

6

Glue on two bottle tops for headlights and a grille from shiny cardstock. This super truck is ready for the road.

BEEP BEEP

Handy Hint

Use clothespins to hold pieces in place while you wait for glue to dry.

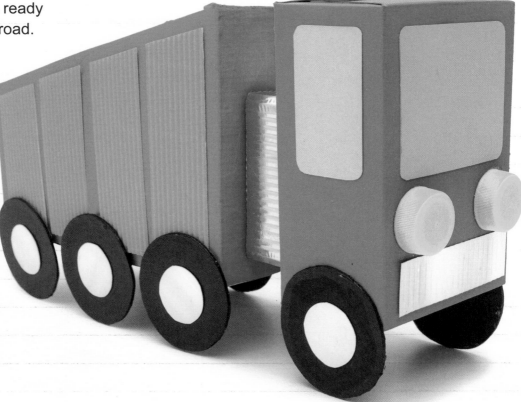

Birdhouse Bank

Count your pennies and save all your money in this colorful birdhouse.

You will need

Tall box
Paint
Cardboard
One straw

1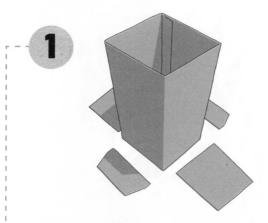

Cut the top flaps off a tall box.

2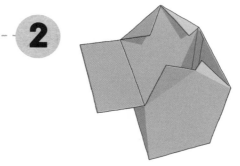

Cut slits in each corner. Fold in the edges to make a triangle at the front and back.

3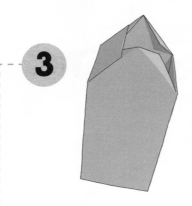

Glue one of the rectangular flaps to the edge of the triangle, as shown. Cut off the other flap.

4

Use a pencil to start a hole for your scissors. Cut out an entrance hole, as shown. Paint the box a bright, pretty color.

5

Cut a rectangle of cardboard and fold it in half to make the roof. Paint it a contrasting color to the birdhouse.

6

Glue one side of the roof to the top of the box. Leave the other side so you can open the box to get your money.

7

Make a hole with a pencil in the front of the box. Glue in a piece of straw for a perch. Now you can start saving your money for something special!

Handy Hint

Make sure the entrance hole in your birdhouse is bigger than your biggest coin.

Fish Tank

If you've always wanted a fish tank, make this fun and colorful water world!

You will need

Rectangular tissue box
Paint, including blue and green
Cardboard
Five googly eyes
Five blue bendy straws

1

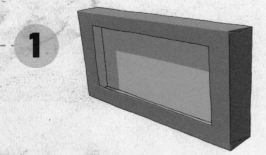

Cut a large, rectangular hole in the front of the tissue box. Paint the inside of the box a light blue and the outside of the box a different shade of blue. This is your fish tank.

2

On cardboard, draw a triangle with a smaller triangle overlapping it, as shown. Then cut it out. This will be one of your fish.

3

Use the template from step 2 to cut out four more fish. Paint the fish bright colors. Glue an eye on to each fish.

4

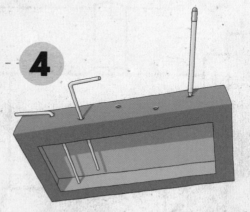

Use a pencil to make five holes in the top of your fish tank. Push a bendy straw through each hole, with the bend at the top.

5

Glue your fish to the straws. Glue them at different heights and facing different directions.

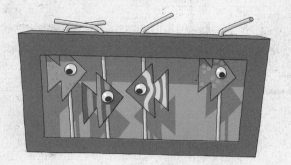

6

To make seaweed, cut out some wavy pieces of cardboard and paint them green. Glue them to the inside of the tank. Twist the straws to make your fish swim.

GLUB GLUB

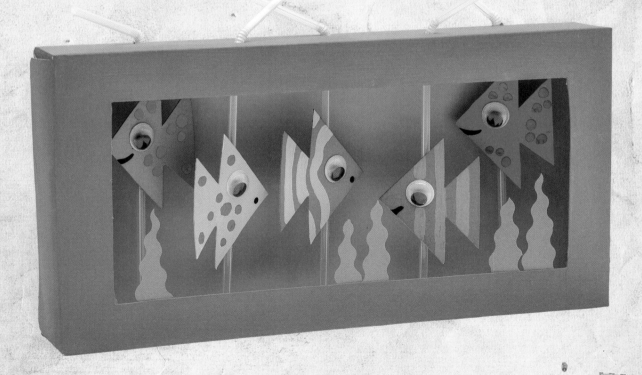

Angelfish

This lovely fish will make your house look heavenly!

You will need

Two cereal boxes
Paint
Yellow cardstock
One googly eye

1

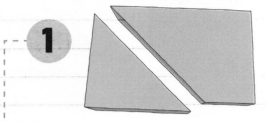

Cut the corner off a box.

2

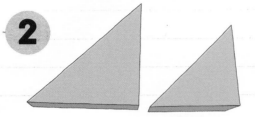

Cut a smaller corner from the other side of the box.

3

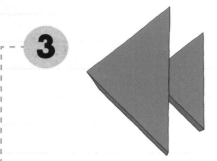

Glue the smaller triangle into the larger one to make a fish shape. Paint the fish and leave it to dry.

4

Paint on spots or stripes.

5

Cut out a circle from yellow cardstock, slightly bigger than the googly eye. Glue the eye to the circle and then glue it to the fish. This colorful fish will brighten up any house.

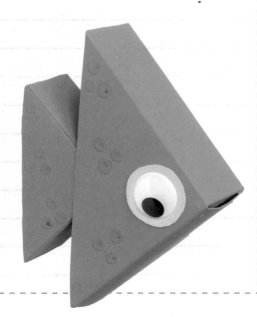

Christmas Tree

You will need

Two cereal boxes
One narrow box
Paint, including green, brown, and yellow
Cardboard

1

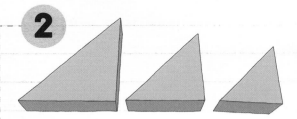

Cut the corner off a box.

2

Cut two corners off another cereal box so that all three triangles are different sizes.

3

Slot the triangles into each other, from the smallest to the biggest. Glue them in place and paint green.

4

Paint a narrow box brown to make the trunk. Glue it to the inside of the bottom triangle.

5

Paint on lots of bright baubles.

6

Cut out a star from the cardboard, paint it yellow, and glue it to the top of your tree. Put your tree on a window ledge to add some festive cheer to your room at Christmastime.

Flower Basket

This flower basket will make a perfect gift for your family and friends. Or maybe just for you!

1 Cut the sides away from a cereal box, as shown.

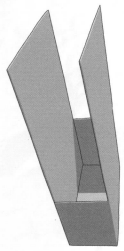

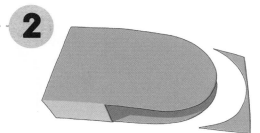

2 Cut away the top to make it curved, as shown.

3 Use a pencil to make a hole for your scissors. Cut out the middle part of the sides to give your basket handles.

4 Paint the handles and cover the bottom part of your basket with corrugated cardstock. Paint the corrugated cardstock to match the handles.

5

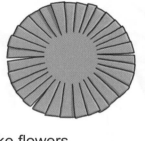

Cut out nine circles from cardstock to make flowers. Cut slits around the edges to create petals. Paint the flowers bright, pretty colors.

6

Add a ball of yellow or orange tissue paper to the center of each flower. Glue a bendy straw to each flower to make a stem.

7

Arrange the flowers in the basket. Push some green tissue paper around the flowers to keep them in place. Your beautiful flowers will brighten up anyone's day!

Handy Hint

If you do not have yellow or orange tissue paper, paint yellow or orange circles instead.

Sitting Dog

This dog will make the perfect pet. Your doggy friend will always sit and beg for attention!

1

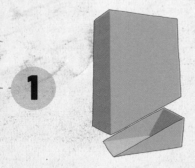

Cut the corner off a cereal box, as shown. Keep the large piece for the body and recycle the rest.

2

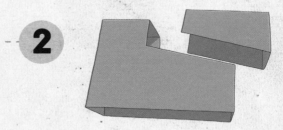

Cut out the head from another cereal box, as shown.

3

Glue the head to the body and paint them both white.

4

Cut out a pair of legs and a tail from cardstock, as shown. Paint them white.

5

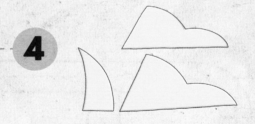

Cut a slit in the back of the body and slide in the tail. Glue to hold in place. Glue the legs to the sides.

6

Cut out a pair of ears from cardstock and paint them black.

7

Glue the ears in place.
Paint a large black
patch on your dog's face.

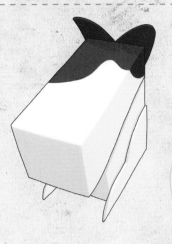

Handy Hint

You can paint on a
nose if you do not
have a bottle top.

8

Add some gray spots. Glue
on a bottle top for the nose
and a pair of googly eyes.
Add a friendly smile.
Woof, woof!

WOOF
WOOF
WOOF

Owl

1

Glue the lid to the base of the box. Paint it a bright color.

You will need

Round box
Paint
Two bottle tops
Cardstock
Cardboard
Two googly eyes

2

Glue two bottle tops so that they stick out off the edge of the box. Cut out two circles from the cardstock so that they are just bigger than the eyes. Glue the eyes to the circles and then the circles to the bottle tops.

3

Cut out a circle of cardstock, paint it, and glue it to the front.

4

Cut out an angled piece of cardstock, as shown. Paint it the same color as the body. Glue to the back of the owl at the top.

5

Cut out a semicircle from cardboard for feet. Cut out a diamond from cardstock for the beak. Paint them yellow.

6

Glue on the beak. Glue the semicircle to the bottom of the box at the back so your owl can stand up. Be a wise owl and decorate your bookshelf!

Treasure Chest

You will need

One shoebox   Yellow cardstock

Paint, including brown   Small boxes

Shiny paper

1 Paint a shoebox brown.

2 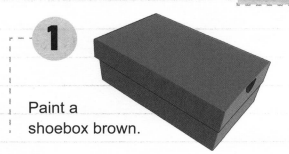 Cut some long narrow strips of yellow cardstock and glue them to the top and front of the box.

3 Cut out a lock from the yellow cardstock.

4 Cut a thin strip of cardstock and glue it to make a loop through the top of the lock. Draw on a keyhole.

5 Glue the lock to the box by gluing on the loop. Add some handles of yellow cardstock to either end. Draw some nails on the chest.

6 Cover some small boxes with shiny paper to make treasure. You could also use your box to keep your favorite things safe.

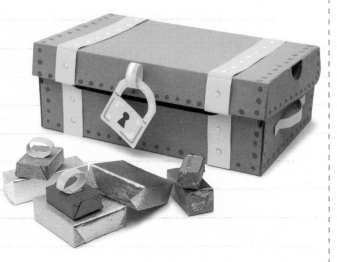

Butterfly

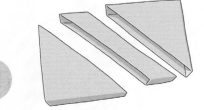

1 Cut the corners off two thin boxes to make the butterfly's wings.

2 Paint the outside of the wings a pretty color and the insides a contrasting color.

3 Place the pieces together so that the ends touch, as shown.

4 Paint a matchbox and glue it on top of the wings for the butterfly's body.

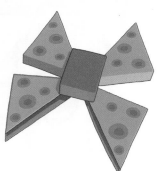

5 Add some spots on the wings.

6 Glue some pieces of straw to the back of the body for antennae. Add two googly eyes and a little smile. You could tie a loop of ribbon to the butterfly and hang it from your ceiling.

Crab

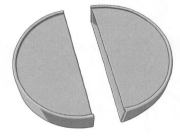

You will need

One round box
Brown and orange paint
Cardboard
Two googly eyes

1

Glue the lid to the base of the box. Cut in half. Paint one half orange.

2

From cardstock, cut two circles slightly bigger than the googly eyes. Paint the circles orange and glue on the eyes.

3

Glue the eyes to the top of the box.

4

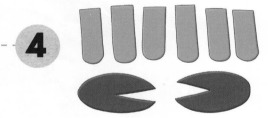

Cut out a pair of claws and six legs from cardboard. Paint the claws brown and the legs orange.

5

Glue the claws to the front of the box. Glue the legs to the inside of the box, so that there are four at the back and two at the front.

6

Add some spots and a mouth. Why not put your crab with the fish from page 22 to make an aquarium?

31

Elephant

Elephants live in a herd so why don't you make your elephant a friend?

1

Cut a triangle in one corner of a cereal box. Cut another triangle on the opposite side. Fold both triangles away from the box, as shown. Cut at the corner from A to B, as shown.

2

Fold the triangles and flaps into the box. Glue to hold in place.

3

Cut out a head shape from the box, as shown.

4

Cut out a semicircle from another box to make the body.

Handy Hint

If you cut the wrong part in step 1, do not worry—you can always tape it back together.

5

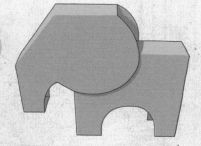

Paint both boxes gray. Glue the head to the body.

6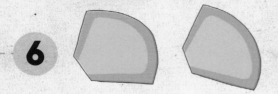

Cut out a pair of ears from cardstock. Paint them gray with pink in the middle.

7

Glue the ears in place.

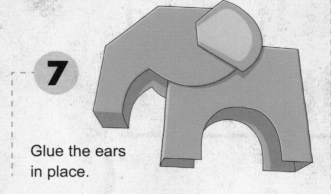

8

Cut out a tail and pair of tusks from the cardstock. Paint the tail gray. Cut out purple circles and glue the eyes to them. Glue on the tail, tusks, and eyes. Paint on some spots and toenails to finish your elephant.

CUTE

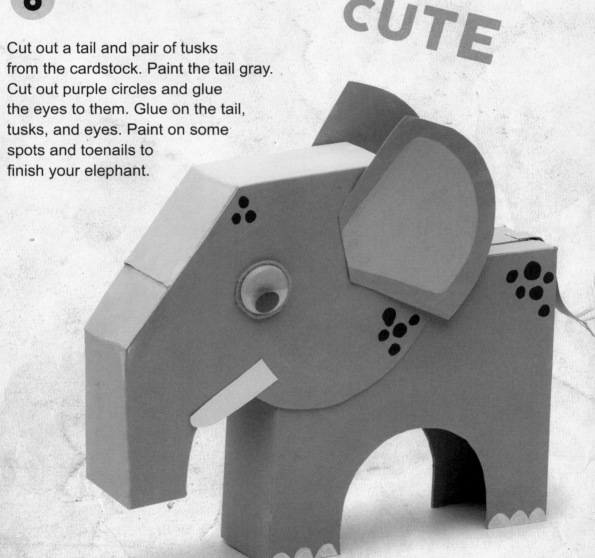

Tiger

Grrrr! Tigers are stripy, orange, and fluffy. But, beware, these cats are anything but cute!

You will need

One cereal box

Orange, black, white, and pink paint

Cardstock

Two googly eyes

One bottle top

1

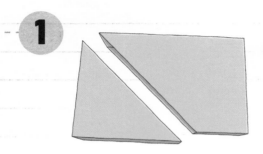

Cut the corner off a cereal box.

2

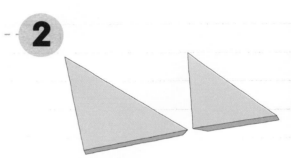

Cut another smaller corner out of the cereal box.

3

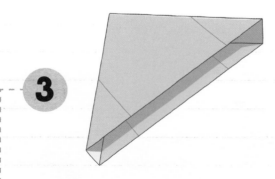

Cut four slits in the larger triangle, as shown. This will be the tiger's body.

4

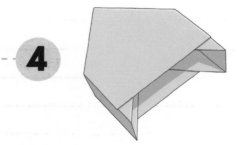

Fold the ends into the middle and glue to hold in place so you have a shape that looks like a house. Cut off any parts that stick out from the bottom so you have a flat base.

5

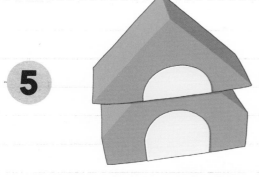

Glue the smaller triangle on top of the bigger one. Paint the tiger orange with a white tummy and muzzle.

6

Cut out a tail and a pair of ears from cardstock. Paint them as shown.

7

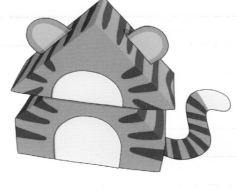

Glue the ears and tail in place. Paint black stripes onto the tiger's body.

GRRR
GRRR

8

Glue on a pair of googly eyes and a bottle top for the nose. Add a mouth to finish off your tiger. Now, your tiger is ready to roar!

Glasses

You will need

**Two square
tissue boxes**

Paint

Cardboard

1

Unfold the boxes
and cut off the tops.

2

Glue the tops together so
that they overlap slightly.
Paint them bright, pretty
colors—you could add
some patterns, too.

3

Cut out a pair of arms
from cardboard and paint
them to match the tops.

4

Turn the glasses over
and glue the arms to
the back, as shown.

5

Bend the arms into
the middle. Your
cool glasses are
ready to wear.

Tractor

Time to get busy on the farm with your tractor. Chug! Chug!

1 Glue the square box to the top of the long box. Paint them both red.

2 Paint the large lids black with white centers to make the back wheels. Cut out two small circles from cardboard and paint them. These are the front wheels.

3 Glue the wheels to the tractor, as shown.

4 Cut out some windows from the cardstock. Glue them to the tractor.

5 Draw a driver and some passengers in the windows. Cut out a rectangle of cardstock and paint it silver to make a grille to attach to the front. Glue the toothpaste tube lid to make the chimney. Your tractor is ready to go!

37

Tulips

Tulips are beautiful, brightly colored flowers. Why not make a bunch of these pretty blooms and put them in a vase?

1 To make two tulips, glue the lid to the base of the round box. Cut it in half.

2 Cut out small triangles to give each half a zig-zag edge.

3 Paint your tulips different colors. Paint the insides too.

4 Use a pencil to make a hole in the bottom of each tulip. Glue a straw into each hole for a stem.

5 Repeat steps 1 to 4 with the second box to make two more tulips. They will make a lovely gift for someone special.

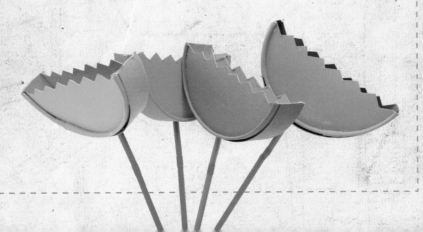

Bunny

1

Paint the box brown.

2

Cut out a pair of feet and ears from cardstock. Paint the feet brown and the ears brown, with pink in the middle.

3

Cut out a dome shape from cardstock for the bunny's tummy. Paint it cream.

4

Glue the ears, feet, and tummy in place.

5

Glue on some googly eyes and draw on a nose and a smile. If you have smaller boxes, you can make some baby bunnies.

39

Penguin

You will need

Chocolate box
Black and blue paint
Cardboard
White and yellow cardstock
Two googly eyes

1

Paint the box black.

2

Cut out a pair of wings from cardboard and paint them black.

3

Next, cut out a dome shape from white cardstock for the penguin's tummy.

4

Glue the wings and tummy in place.

5

Cut out two circles from the white cardstock. Paint them blue and glue the eyes to them. Glue the eyes in place.

6

Cut out a beak from yellow cardstock and glue it under the eyes. Your penguin is ready to swim.

Row of Houses Desk Bins

1 You will need two boxes the same size for each house. To make each house, cut off the corner of one of the boxes, for the roof.

2 Fold the top flaps inside and glue to hold in place. This will make it stronger when you take the roof on and off. Paint the house.

3 Glue some corrugated cardstock to the roof and paint it.

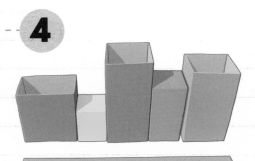

4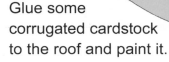

Now repeat steps 1 to 3 with the other boxes, but have some solid boxes, with closed tops, between the open ones. Glue the row of houses onto a strip of cardboard.

5 Put the roofs on the open-ended boxes. Cut out rectangles for windows and glue them to your houses. Put all your pens and pencils in the houses to keep your desk neat and tidy.

Mice and Cheese

Do mice love cheese? You bet! And you'll love these little mice and the cheese once you've made them!

You will need

Two cereal boxes

Gray, black, and dark and light yellow paint

Pink cardstock

Four googly eyes

1

To make each mouse, cut the corner off a box so that the cut piece has three edges. This will be the body.

2

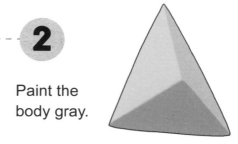

Paint the body gray.

3

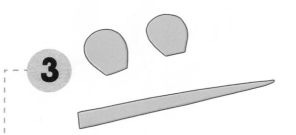

Cut out a pair of ears and a tail from pink cardstock.

4

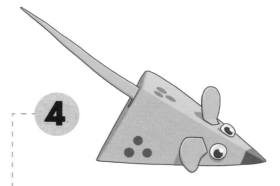

Glue the tail and ears to the body, paint on a black nose and some spots. Glue on a pair of googly eyes. Repeat the steps to make another mouse, but paint it a darker color.

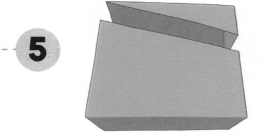

5 Cut the top off another box, at an angle—you need the small piece for your wedge of cheese. Recycle the rest.

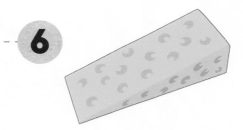

6 Paint the cheese yellow. Paint on some crescents with a darker yellow to look like holes.

7 Place your mice on the cheese and let them nibble away!

Handy Hint
Have a game of cat and mouse when you make these mice and the cat from page 51.

SQUEAK

Crown

This crown is fit for a Queen...or a King!

1

Gently flatten a cereal box and cut it in half.

2

Cut out a row of triangles around one edge of the top half.

3

Paint your crown yellow.

4

Cut a strip of cardstock to fit around the bottom of the crown. Paint it gold and glue it in place.

5

Cut out some circles from cardstock and paint them jewel-like colors. Add some glitter to the centers.

6

Glue the jewels to the tips of the crown and it will be fit for royalty!

spider

1

Paint your box black.
This will be the spider's body.

2

Cut out eight
legs from cardboard.
Paint them black.

3

Glue the legs to the
base of the body.

4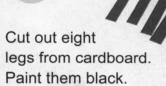

Turn over your spider and
bend the legs, as shown.

5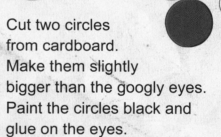

Cut two circles
from cardboard.
Make them slightly
bigger than the googly eyes.
Paint the circles black and
glue on the eyes.

6

Glue the eyes to
the body. Paint
on spots. Is your
spider friendly
or scary?

Snail

You will need

Round box
Paint
Cardboard
Two pompoms

One bendy straw
Two googly eyes

1 Paint the lid and base of a round box.

2 Cut off part of the rim from the base of the box, as shown.

3 Cut out a body for your snail from cardboard. Paint it then glue the body onto the cut-out part of the box base.

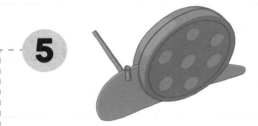

4 Glue the lid to the base, so that the body is trapped between the lid and the base. Paint on some spots.

5 Use the tip of a pencil to make a hole in the head. Insert a piece of bendy straw into the hole for the horns.

6 Glue some pompoms to the horns. Draw on a smile and a pair of googly eyes. Cute!

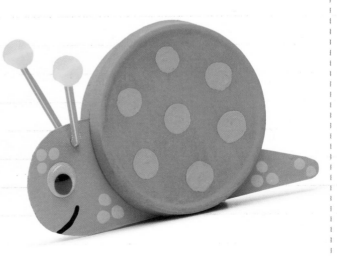

Octopus

1

Paint the top of your box green and the underside pink. This will be the body.

2

Cut out eight legs from cardstock. Paint them green on one side and pink on the other.

3

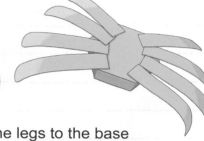

Glue the legs to the base of the body, pink side up.

4

Cut two circles from cardstock. Make them slightly bigger than the googly eyes. Paint the circles green and glue on the eyes.

5

Turn your octopus over and gently curl his legs upward. Glue on his eyes.

6

Paint on lots of spots and a smile. Your octopus is ready—why not put him in your bathroom?

Chickens

Cluck, cluck! Who's the cutest chicken on the farm? I think these two are in the running!

You will need

Two cereal boxes

Brown, yellow, white, and gray paint

Red and yellow cardstock

Four googly eyes

1

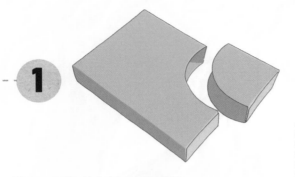

For each chicken, cut the corner off a box, making the base curved.

2

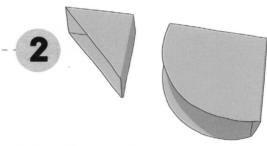

Cut another smaller corner, with a straight base.

3

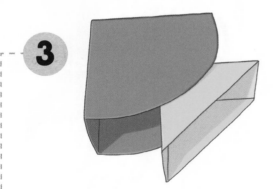

Paint the curved corner brown for the body, and the small one yellow for the feet. Glue the feet to the inside of the body.

4

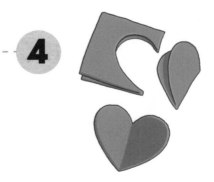

Cut out two crests from red cardstock.

5

Cut out a beak from yellow cardstock.

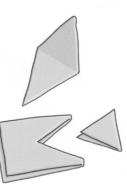

6

Glue the crests and beak in place.

7

Add a pair of googly eyes and some gray spots. Repeat the steps to make the second chicken, but paint its body white instead of brown.

Handy Hint

Always allow the glue to dry completely before moving your model.

CLUCK CLUCK

Picnic Basket

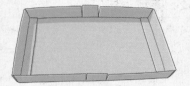

1 Cut two slits in either side of the shoebox lid.

2 Fold the lid back on itself along each slit. Use the edge of a table to make a straight crease.

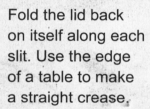

3 Paint the lid and the base of the box green. Paint some flowers on the base.

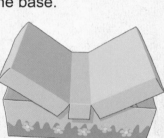

4 Cut and fold a strip of cardboard to make a handle. Make sure that it fits over the lid of the box.

5 Glue the middle of the lid to the base—you should still be able to open the lid from each end.

6 Decorate the lid and glue the handle in place. Happy picnicking!

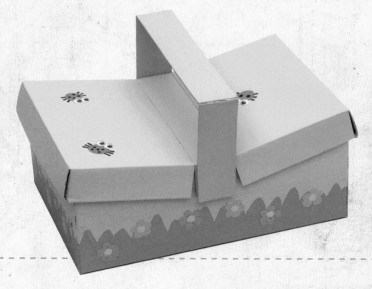

Cool Cat

You will need

Chocolate box
Orange, yellow, and pink paint
Cardboard
White cardstock
Pink felt
Two googly eyes

1

Paint the box yellow.

2

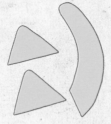

Cut out a pair of ears and a tail from cardboard and paint yellow.

3

Paint the middle of the ears pink. Glue them and the tail in place.

4

Cut out a dome shape from white cardstock for the cat's tummy. Glue it to the front of the box. Paint some stripes onto the rest of the box.

5

Cut out a semicircle of pink felt for the cat's nose. Glue the nose and a pair of eyes to the face. Draw on a mouth. If you have some smaller boxes, you can make some cute kittens.

51

Robot Mask

Robots at the ready! Look out, here we come! Make this awesome robot mask and take the world by storm.

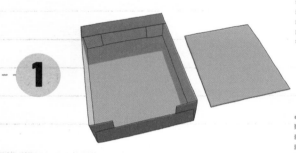

1 Cut the back off a cereal box. Paint the front of the box blue.

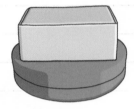

2 Glue the lids to the bases of two round boxes. Paint the boxes red. Cover two small boxes with shiny cardstock. Glue one to each of the round boxes.

3 Glue the small boxes to either side of the mask, as shown. Use the end of a pencil to make a hole for your scissors, then cut out two circles on the front of the box for eye holes. Paint white circles around them.

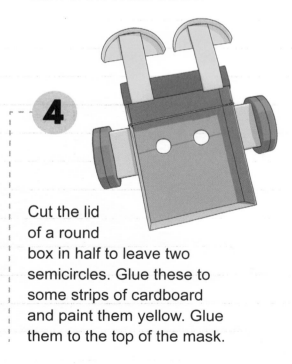

4 Cut the lid of a round box in half to leave two semicircles. Glue these to some strips of cardboard and paint them yellow. Glue them to the top of the mask.

5

Add some colored bottle tops above the eyes.

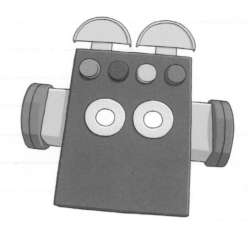

6

To make the mouth, cover a small box with shiny cardstock and glue it in place. Your robot mask is ready to wear.

ROBOTS RULE

Handy Hint

To keep your mask in place, make holes on either side of the mask and attach some elastic.

Reindeer

This amazing reindeer is every bit as cute as Rudolf! Have fun making a whole team of reindeer to pull your sleigh.

You will need

Two cereal boxes
One small box
Brown, white, and pink paint
Cardstock
Two googly eyes
Black bottle top
White pompom

1 Cut out the body shape from a cereal box, as shown.

2 Cut the end off a small box to make a cube for the reindeer's neck.

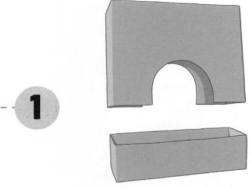

3 Cut the corner from another cereal box for the head.

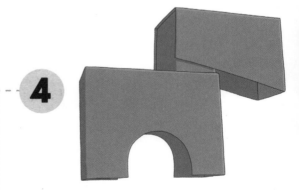

4 Glue the neck to the body and then glue on the head. Paint the whole reindeer brown.

5

Cut out a pair of ears and a pair of antlers. Paint them all brown.

6

Glue on the ears and antlers. Add a bottle top for the nose.

7

Paint on some white spots. Add pink to the middle of the ears. Glue on a pair of eyes and a pompom for the tail. Draw on a smile and your reindeer is ready.

CUTE

Robot

Make an army of super-cool robots to take over the world! (Or just your house.)

You will need

- Two different sized boxes
- Paint
- Two toilet tubes
- Two matchboxes
- Corrugated cardstock
- Two candy tubes
- Thin cardstock
- Shiny paper
- Two metal fasteners
- Two bendy straws
- Four bottle tops
- Googly eyes
- Three tube tops

1

Paint two different sized boxes. Then glue the smaller box to the top of the larger box.

2

Glue two toilet tubes covered with corrugated cardstock to the base of the large box for legs.

3

Next, paint two matchboxes and glue them to the toilet tubes. These will be the feet.

4

To make each arm, cut the end off a candy tube and paint it. Cut out two circles of cardstock and paint them. Use a metal fastener to attach the open end of the arms to the circles of colored cardstock.

5

Glue the arms to either side of the body, as shown. You will be able to move the arms up and down.

6

Use the end of a pencil to make two holes at the top of the head. Insert two small pieces of bendy straw. Cut a rectangle of shiny paper for the front and glue in place.

7

Glue on some bottle tops for the eyes and ears. Add some googly eyes to the inside of the bottle tops and a strip of painted corrugated cardstock for a mouth.

8

Glue some tube tops and colored cardstock circles to the robot's tummy to decorate it. Your robot is complete—have lots of fun playing with it!

zebra

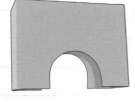

1

Cut out the body from one of the boxes, as shown.

2

Cut the end off the small box to make a cube for the neck.

3

Cut the corner from the other box for the head.

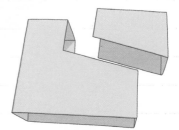

4

Glue the neck to the body and then glue on the head. Paint the zebra white with black stripes and a black nose.

5

Cut out a pair of ears, a mane, and a tail from black cardstock. Glue them in place.

6

Cut out some circles of cardstock that are slightly bigger than the googly eyes. Glue the eyes to the circles and add them to the zebra. Paint on a mouth and two nostrils.

Whale

You'll have a whale of a time making this beautiful sea giant!

You will need

One shoebox with a detachable lid

Paint

One cardboard box

Cardstock

Two googly eyes

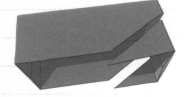

1

Paint the base of the shoebox dark blue on the outside and pink on the inside. Cut the end of the base diagonally, as shown.

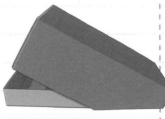

2

Paint the lid pale blue on the outside and pink on the inside. Glue the base to the lid so that it is open, as shown.

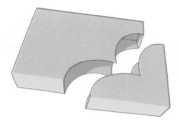

3

Cut out a heart-shaped corner from the other box. This will be the tail.

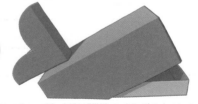

4

Paint the tail dark blue and glue it to the body.

5

Cut out some circles of cardstock. Paint a contrasting color. Glue the eyes to the circles and attach to the whale's head. Paint on some spots to finish your whale.

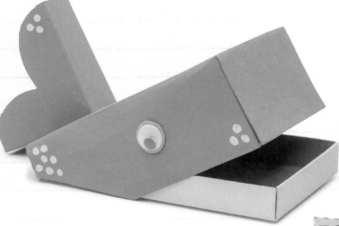

Bug Bracelet

You will need

Four matchboxes
Cardboard ring from a finished roll of tape
Paint
Black felt
Eight googly eyes

1

Paint your matchboxes different colors.

2

Cut six narrow strips of black felt and glue to the base of each box for legs.

3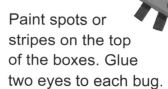

Paint spots or stripes on the top of the boxes. Glue two eyes to each bug.

4

Paint the cardboard tape ring green.

5

Glue the bugs to the outside of the cardboard ring to make a bracelet. To make a ring for your finger instead, glue a small loop of cardboard to the back of a bug.

Frog

You will need

One box with
a hinged lid
Cardboard
Green and yellow paint
Two googly eyes

1

Cut out a semicircle of cardstock the same width as the box. Glue the semicircle to the front of the lid and paint green, as shown.

2

Paint on a yellow tummy.

3

Cut out two small semicircles and paint them green. Glue them to the front of the box for the feet.

4

From cardstock, cut two circles slightly bigger than the eyes. Paint the circles green and glue on the eyes.

5

Bend the bottom of the cardstock circles and glue the eyes to the top of the box.

6

Paint on yellow spots and a happy smile. Be careful your frog doesn't hop away!

61

Dinosaur

Dinosaurs lived around 230 million years ago but you can make this super dino today!

1

Cut a corner off the large cereal box for the dinosaur's body. Keep the rest of the box, to make a tail and legs.

2

Cut a long triangle from the leftover pieces of cereal box to make the dinosaur tail.

3

Cut a slot halfway up one side of the body, and slide in the tail. Glue to hold in place.

4

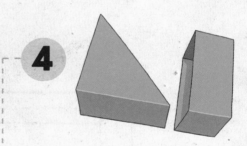

Cut a corner and end section from the small cereal box to make the head and neck.

5

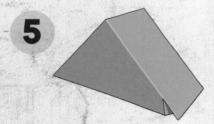

Cut two small slits at one end of the triangle from step 4, and fold in. Glue in place. This is the snout.

6

Glue the neck into the head.

7

Cut four triangles from corrugated cardstock for the legs.

Handy Hint

Use a piece of cardstock as a spatula to spread the glue.

8

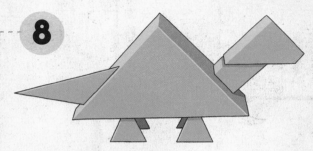

Glue the head, neck, and legs in place. Let them dry. Paint and decorate the dinosaur. Glue some small triangles from felt for its spine. Use two felt circles for the googly eyes and fix in place. Now your dinosaur is ready to roar!

Monster Photo Frame

You will need

One tissue box
Paint
Thin cardstock
Two googly eyes
White felt

1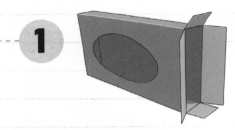

Open one end of the tissue box. If the front has any plastic in it, remove it now.

Handy Hint
You can use thin cardstock if you don't have felt.

2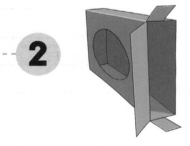

To make a slot to slide your photo through, cut off one of the long flaps and around ½ inch off the small flaps on either side. Glue the remaining parts back together.

3

Cut two circles from the cardstock. They need to be slightly larger than the googly eyes.

4

Paint the circles and your box.

5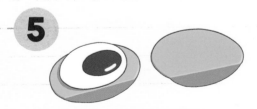

Once dry, fold the bottom part of the cardstock circles, as shown. Then glue the eyes in place.

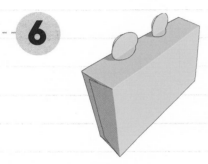

6

Glue the folded edge of each circle to the long side of the tissue box, with the eyes facing forward.

7

Cut lots of teeth from felt and glue them around the inside of the mouth. Decorate your monster, then choose a sassy little monster photo to pop inside!

BOO!

Piglet

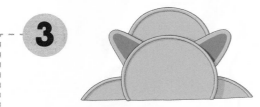

1

Glue the lid and base of one box together. Then cut the base and lid from the other box, as shown. Glue the larger piece's lid and base together but do not glue the small pieces. Paint all pieces pink.

You will need

Two round boxes

Light and dark pink paint

Pink and blue cardstock

Two googly eyes

One bottle top

2

Glue the two small pieces to the base of the whole box. These will be the pig's trotters.

3

Cut out a pair of ears from cardstock and paint them. Glue the ears to the top of the head, and fold the tips forward. Glue the head to the pig's body, as shown.

4

Paint a bottle top pink and glue it to the pig's face.

5

Wrap a strip of pink cardstock around a pencil to make a curly tail.

6

From blue cardstock, cut two circles slightly bigger than the eyes. Glue them, the googly eyes, and the tail in place. Paint on nostrils.

Ladybug Box

You will need

One round box
Cardboard
Black, red, and blue paint
Two googly eyes
Two metal fasteners

1

Cut the lid from the round box into slightly less than half. Recycle the bigger piece. Paint the smaller piece and the base of the box black.

2

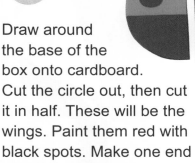

Draw around the base of the box onto cardboard. Cut the circle out, then cut it in half. These will be the wings. Paint them red with black spots. Make one end black, for the head.

3

Make a hole with the tip of a pencil through the wing and the lid section. Use a metal fastener to attach together. Repeat with the other wing.

4

Glue the lid to the base, but do not get any glue on the wings.

5

From cardboard, cut out circles that are slightly bigger than the eyes. Paint them blue and glue on a pair of googly eyes. Cut six legs from cardboard and paint black. Glue the eyes and legs to the ladybug.

Castle

If you like stories with knights and princesses or dungeons and dragons, you'll love this amazing castle!

You will need

About seven or eight different sized boxes, including one with an opening flap

Paint

Cardstock

Two straws

1

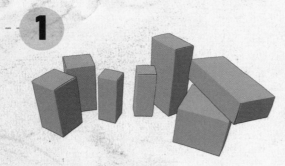

Paint the boxes and leave to dry.

2

The box with the opening flap will be the drawbridge. Paint the inside of this a contrasting color.

3

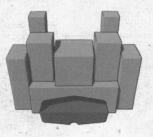

Glue all your boxes together in a castle shape.

4

Cut some narrow strips of cardstock. Then cut small notches along one edge of the strips of cardstock.

5

Glue these strips of cardstock to the top edges of the boxes, as shown.

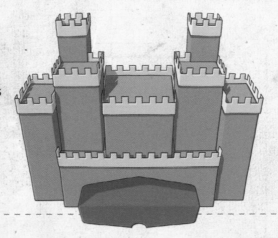

6

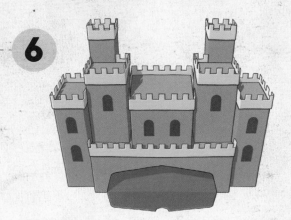

Cut out some windows from cardstock. Paint and glue in place.

7

Make some flags by cutting and painting cardstock. Then glue them to short pieces of straws, as shown.

8

In the top of the towers, make a hole for each flag. Glue in place. Your castle is ready to play with!

Handy Hint

Practice arranging your castle before you glue the boxes together.

Big Mouth Monster

This monster has a BIG MOUTH. Make your monster scary or funny—you decide!

You will need

One box with an opening flap

Paint

Two matchboxes

White cardstock

Three googly eyes

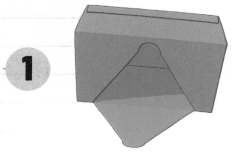

1 You need a box with an opening flap on it. Paint it a bright color on the outside and a different color on the inside.

2 Paint two matchboxes. These will be the feet.

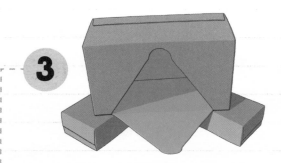

3 Glue the monster's body to the feet. Make sure the flap is at the front.

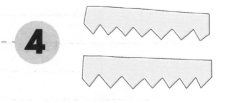

4 Cut two narrow strips of white cardstock. Then cut out triangles along one edge of the strips. These will be the teeth.

5

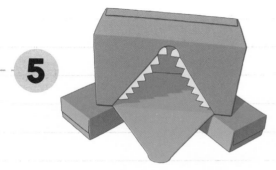

Glue the teeth to the inside of the top of the mouth, as shown.

6

Cut three circles from cardstock. They should be slightly bigger than the googly eyes. Paint the circles the same color as the body, and glue on the eyes.

7

Glue the eyes to the top of the box. Paint on some spots and toenails. Your monster is ready to scare your friends!

ARRR

Lion

Lions live in groups called a pride. How many lions will you make?

1 Glue the lid and base of one box together. Then cut the base and lid from the other box, as shown. Glue the larger piece's lid and base together but do not glue the small pieces. Paint all pieces yellow.

2 Cut out a pair of ears and a tail from cardboard. Paint as shown.

3 Glue the ears to the top of the round box.

4 Cut out a strip of brown felt. Cut a fringe along one edge to make the lion's mane.

5 Glue the mane around the back edge of the head. Glue the head to the large piece of the cut box, as shown.

6 Glue the two small pieces of the cut box to the body for the paws.

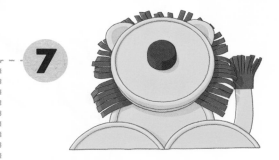

7 Stick a piece of the fringed felt to the end of the tail. Glue this and a bottle-top nose in place.

8 Cut green circles of felt that are slightly bigger than the googly eyes. Glue them to the lion's face, and glue the eyes to them. Add a smile and ROAR... your lion is ready to play.

ROAR ROAR

Parrot

Who's a clever bird, then?
This parrot and its friend!
Make these jungle birds and
put them in your bedroom.

You will need

Four boxes

Two long, narrow boxes

Paint, including black and brown

White cardboard

Two googly eyes

1

For each parrot, cut the side of a box as shown. You need the top part for the parrot's body.

2

Cut a curved corner off another box to make the parrot's head.

3

Paint the pieces and glue them together.

4

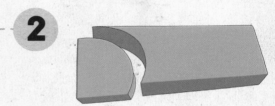

Cut out a beak from cardboard and paint it black.

5

Cut a slit in the front of the head, slide in the beak, and glue to hold.

6

Cut out a pair of wings from cardboard and paint feathers, as shown.

7

Glue on the wings. Cut out two circles from the cardstock and glue them to either side of the head. Glue on a pair of googly eyes, as shown.

8

Paint around the eyes and add detail to the beak. Paint the narrow box brown. Glue the box into the middle of the body so the parrot has a perch. Repeat all the steps to make the second parrot— why not paint it in different colors?

Handy Hint
Cut the perches at different heights so the birds look like they are on different trees.

Crane

Building sites are busy, busy, busy! Can you build a crane to help lift the heavy loads?

You will need

Small cereal box

Paint

Three narrow boxes

Corrugated cardstock

Eight bottle tops

Cardstock

Two bendy straws

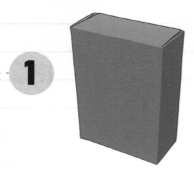

1 Paint a small cereal box.

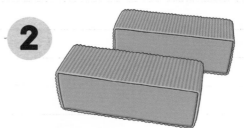

2 Paint two narrow boxes in a different color. Glue a strip of corrugated cardstock around four edges of each box, as shown.

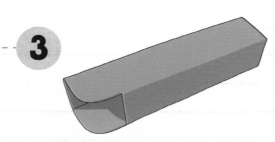

3 Cut the end of another narrow box, as shown. Paint it to match the other boxes in step 2.

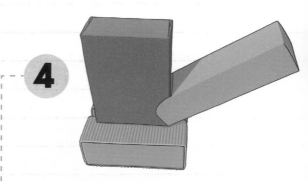

4 Glue the narrow boxes to the blue box, as shown.

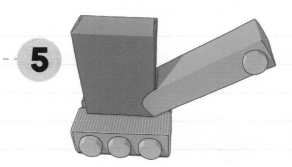

5

Glue on the bottle tops for the track rollers and the crane winch.

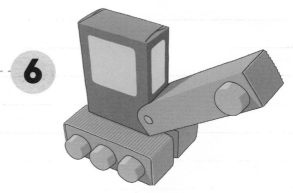

6

Cut out some windows from cardstock and glue onto the cab. Add a dot of paint for the screw on the winch.

7

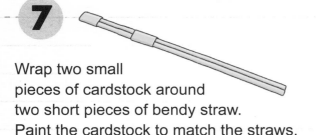

Wrap two small pieces of cardstock around two short pieces of bendy straw. Paint the cardstock to match the straws.

8

Make a hole in the base of the crane arm with the tip of a pencil. Glue the straws in place to make the crane grab. Get ready, steady, build!

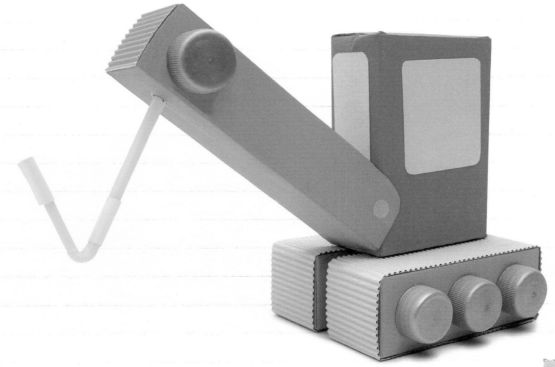

Pirate Ship

Arrggh! Calling all pirates! Prepare to set sail on the seven seas in this pirate ship.

You will need

One cereal box

Two boxes of different sizes

Brown, yellow, blue, red, black, and white paint

Cardstock, including gray

Cardboard

1 Carefully open the ends of a large cereal box. Cut off the flaps, as shown.

2 Cut a slit down one edge and fold back the side at an angle. Repeat on all four of the base corners.

3 Fold the corners in and bring the base and top sides together. Glue to hold in place. This will give you a ship-shaped base.

4 Paint the shaped box brown.

5 Paint two different sized boxes brown and glue them to the large box, as shown.

6 Cut out lots of circles of cardstock and paint as portholes. Glue them to the sides.

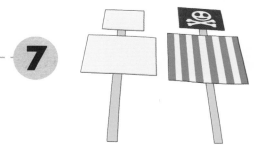

7

Cut out some sails from cardstock and paint them. Cut out some narrow strips of cardboard for the masts and paint yellow. Glue the sails to the masts.

8

Fold a piece of gray cardstock in half and cut out an anchor. Glue the anchor to the ship.

9

Make slits in the top box with a pencil and glue in the masts. Your pirate ship is ready to sail—arrggh, me hearties, land ahoy!

Handy Hint

Why not design your own flag to fly on your pirate ship?

Quarto is the authority on a wide range of topics.
Quarto educates, entertains and enriches the lives of
our readers—enthusiasts and lovers of hands-on living.
www.quartoknows.com

Design and Editorial: Calcium
Photography: Michael Wicks
Illustration: Tom Connell
With thanks to our wonderful models Islah, Ethan and Ania.

First published in the United States in 2016
by QEB Publishing, Inc.
Part of The Quarto Group
6 Orchard
Lake Forest, CA 92630

A CIP record for this book is available from the Library of Congress.

ISBN 978 1 60992 834 6

Printed in China